Richard Morgan
Well Done!*

D0489310

C152936307

I can dress
to play
outside...

...all by myself.

I can ride
my bike
to go
and hide...

Well done!

I can wash my face
in time for tea...

I can
scoop up peas
on a spoon
for me...

...all by
myself.

I can hold on,

so I don't miss...

...all by
myself.

I can hug and
I can kiss,
but I need
YOU
to do this!

I like to try and do things
all by myself. Sometimes, though,
I get things a little wrong.
Now and then, I get things a lot
wrong... But by trying, I grow
a lot and this makes my mummy
and daddy very happy.
And then I can do
even more things
ALL BY MYSELF!

Charlie
x

For Isobel,
the non-stop chatterbox.